the fitness food cookbook

p

This is a Parragon Publishing Book
First published in 2006

Parragon Publishing
Queen Street House
4 Queen Street
Bath, BA1 1HE, UK

ISBN: 1-40546-551-4

Printed in China

Author: Fiona Biggs
Cover Photographer: Karen Thomas

Notes for the Reader
Cup measurements in this book are for American cups. This book also uses imperial and
metric measurements. Follow the same units of measurement throughout; do not mix imperial
and metric. All spoon measurements are level: teaspoons are assumed to be 5 ml and
tablespoons are assumed to be 15 ml. Unless otherwise stated, milk is assumed to be whole
milk, eggs and individual vegetables such as potatoes are medium, and pepper is freshly
ground black pepper. The times given for each recipe are an approximate guide only because
the preparation times may differ according to the techniques used by different people and the
cooking times may vary as a result of the type of oven used. Recipes using raw or very lightly
cooked eggs should be avoided by infants, the elderly, pregnant women, convalescents, and
anyone suffering from an illness.

contents

introduction: a well balanced diet

The cliché that you are what you eat contains more than a grain of truth. However, it must also be said that you are just as much how you eat and even when you eat.

Food providing a balanced intake of essential nutrients and energy, that is calories, tell only part of the story. There are also nutrients in food that help protect against disease and still others that play an important role in maintaining the body's systems in peak condition. Equally, there are nutrients in food which, taken in excess over a period of time, can do long-term, sometimes irreversible damage.

And if that's not enough to think about, how and when you eat are also essential considerations for eating well. There is an old saying that you should breakfast like a king, lunch like a prince, and dine like a pauper. Research during the last decades, as well as anecdotal evidence, certainly seem to bear this out although not, perhaps, in quite such an extreme form. Schools report that children who eat an energizing breakfast and a well-balanced lunch are better behaved, more attentive, and work harder throughout the entire day. Most of us know that if we skip breakfast because there isn't time or we just can't be bothered, then we are far more likely to succumb to the temptation of unhealthy and unsatisfying sugary or salty snacks in the middle of the morning.

We are probably also all familiar with the downward spiral of fluctuating blood-sugar levels and energy levels that is only ever temporarily halted by nibbling a bar of chocolate. Applying the principles of the glycemic index (GI) diet can help maintain even blood sugar levels throughout the day. Low–GI foods, such as apples, oatmeal, and spaghetti are digested slowly, keeping blood sugar levels more stable (and ensuring that you stay feeling full for longer). Medium–GI foods, such as new potatoes, raw pineapple, orange juice and multi-grain breads, are digested more quickly, and high–GI foods, such as pretzels, cereal bars, cornflakes and white rice will provide instant energy in the short-term with rapid rise in blood glucose. The key to the diet is to choose most of your food from the list of low–GI staples, and indulge in medium– and high–GI foods in moderation.

What you eat

If all this sounds very complicated and suggests that you have to eat unbelievably boring meals, live to a rigid schedule, and ban certain foods, don't despair. That simply is not the case.

Firstly, healthy dishes are actually among the most delicious and tempting. It hardly needs saying that the freshest ingredients are the ones with the best flavor and texture, as well as the highest levels of nutrients. The easiest way to ensure a balanced diet is to include lots of different food types and, therefore, lots of exciting variety in the week's menus. Just a quick glance through some of the recipes in this book will quickly reassure you that healthy eating truly means eating well. From Chili Bean Cakes with Avocado Salsa to Beef Stew with Garlic & Shallots you are sure to find tempting dishes to please all the family. Even kids, who can sometimes be quite fussy eaters, find Banana Breakfast Shake, Tuna Kabobs, and Fruit & Nut Squares hard to resist.

All these fabulous recipes are easy to follow with step–by–step instructions. In addition, each one includes an at–a–glance guide to its specific nutritional content with information on the quantities of carbohydrates, fats, and proteins, as well as a calorie count per serving. More detail is provided by separately listing the sugar content and amount of saturated fat-watchpoints in any healthy eating plan. To make it even easier to understand the specific nutritional advantages of any particular recipe a "color dot" guide will alert you to its "Eat Well" category or categories. The health benefits of these categories are described below.

When you eat

So, you don't have to have a masters degree in human nutrition to eat well–this book makes it simple, rather than complicated. Equally, it is obvious from the recipes that healthy meals are far from boring. It will, therefore, be no surprise to discover that this book also helps you find a flexible way to incorporate a regular pattern of healthy eating into a busy 21st–century lifestyle. The first three chapters provide recipes for the three main meals of the day–breakfast, lunch, and dinner–to help you maintain a balanced intake of nutrients to optimize both physical and mental health throughout the day.

Choose most of your food from the list of low GI staples, and indulge in medium and high GI foods in moderation.

A good start to the day is essential for all the family and eating breakfast provides the energy boost needed to get going and re-energize the body after a night fasting. The recipes in Kick–Start the Day are easy to prepare and most are very quick, as mornings are usually a rush for most families. Carbohydrate-rich foods, such as cereals and toast, provide slow-release energy and are ideal breakfast foods. Fruit, too, features in many of the recipes – an easy way to increase the family's intake to the recommended five a day. Light & Lively Lunches provides recipes for quick, easy, wholesome, and satisfying dishes to top up the energy levels and keep you going, whether a bowl of tasty homemade soup, a variation on the traditional omelet, or a flavor-packed salad. There are even recipes for great light bites to take to work. Desirable Dinners is full of marvelous ideas for the family's main meal of the day-appetizers, mains, and desserts–delicious, satisfying, and packed with goodness. There has never been a better reason to gather around the table and share each other's news while finalizing the day's energy intake. However, even these ideas are flexible as, although most families eat their main meal in the evening these days, if your lifestyle would work better by swapping Light & Lively Lunches and Desirable Dinners, there is absolutely no reason why you shouldn't do so.

However, life doesn't always run according to plan and there are times when a "little something" to fill the gap is essential. Consequently, the final chapter, Healthier Treats, offers recipes for just such occasions-delicious, but healthy snacks for when you need to eat on the run, when the kids have just come home from school, when the entire family is freezing cold and ravenous after a Saturday afternoon game, or when your meeting overran by two hours. These range from quick and easy fruity combinations to savory spreads and satisfying bakes.

Watchpoints

When it comes to banning foods, many of us are all too well aware that the moment certain foods are forbidden, they are immediately magically transformed into irresistible items of desire. This is why the emphasis throughout Fitness Food is on healthy balance including fabulous, flavor-packed, nutritional ingredients rather than avoiding specific food groups. That said, there is no denying that modern research has demonstrated that certain products can be quite harmful, especially if eaten to excess.

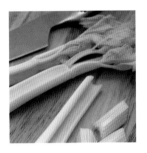

Maintaining a balanced intake of nutrients will help you optimize both physical and mental health throughout the day.

Eating fruit need not be boring - check out our delicious Vitality Boosters for healthy snacks on the run.

Nowadays, most people are aware that the Western diet tends to contain too much fat and that the type that really does the damage is saturated fat, which usually comes from animal sources. A diet with a disproportionate amount of fat can make you gain weight, if there is a high proportion of saturated fat, it can increase blood cholesterol and the risk of heart disease. This is as serious for children as it is for adults, and can establish an unhealthy pattern of eating for life. Following the recipes in Fitness Food is an easy way to ensure that none of the family is eating too much fat and, equally important, that everyone is getting the right amount of 'good' fats. In addition, for those who think they may have been a little too generous with the fats in the past, there are a number of lowfat recipes to help launch your healthy eating plan.

Sugar is another temptation that is hard to resist and, of course, the occasional sweet treat will cause no real harm. Although sugar is a source of calories there are no other nutrients. It is also bad for the teeth. Consuming sugar provides a sudden energy surge, followed soon after by an equally abrupt dip in energy. The natural sugar found in fruit is broken down more slowly than processed or refined sugar as it comes 'packaged' with nutrients which helps the body to process it. Instead of providing the body with vitamins and minerals, refined sugar actually uses up precious micro-nutrients to process it. Turn to the sweet recipes in Fitness Food, most of them based on fresh or dried fruit and all of them delicious.

High levels of salt in the diet are thought to be associated with high blood pressure and increased risk of stroke. The recipes in Fitness Food have cleverly substituted other ways of providing additional flavor, from spicy marinades to sprinkling the cooked dish with fresh herbs, so no one will even notice the much lower or even non-existent salt level. And, of course, when you are in charge of the cooking, you are also fully in control of how much or how little salt you add.

Sensible guidelines, such as eating only moderate amounts of dairy foods, are not always easy to follow-how much is moderate and is it the same amount when applied to heavy cream as lowfat yogurt? Fitness Food has been compiled in line with modern nutritional recommendations and provides easily accessible nutritional data, so you don't have to give yourself a headache trying to find the answers to such questions.

Fitness Food categories

These categories highlight special features in the recipes, from specific ingredients that are particularly beneficial to health, to low levels of ingredients that are not or, at least, not if eaten in excess. Many of the recipes fall into a number of categories, demonstrating just how easy it is to eat well.

Some categories, such as lowfat, are self-explanatory. You can check the exact fat content-both saturated and unsaturated-in the nutritional information of each flagged recipe. Recipes are assigned a 'lowfat' icon (see icons, below right) if they contain 3g fat per serving or less. Other categories may be vaguely familiar, but slightly puzzling.

The five-a-day category refers to fruit and vegetables, which are highly nutritious and very rich in vitamins and minerals. They contain very little fat, few calories, and are often a good source of fiber. In addition, many contain naturally occurring chemicals that may help to protect against such diseases as cancer and heart disease. 'Five a Day' icons are given to are recipes which contribute to the recommended daily intake of five pieces of fruit and vegetables. One serving of fruit or vegetables is considered to be 80g and any contribution to the daily recommendation is marked with an icon.

Omega-3 is a "good" fat and, in fact, it helps maintain a strong and healthy heart and circulatory system. The National Institutes of Health recommends that people consume at least 2% of their total daily calories as omega 3 fats. The Omega-3 icon appears against any recipe that contains foods which contribute to the advised intake. These foods are flaxseeds and walnuts, soybeans, navy beans, or kidney beans, tofu, fish, winter squash, and olive oil.

The Glycemic Index rates carbohydrate foods from 100 to 0 and measures the rise in blood sugar levels that is caused by each one. All foods are compared to the effect pure glucose has on blood glucose which is given an arbitrary figure of 100. Low GI foods take longer to absorb and keep blood sugar levels more constant. Low GI foods are considered to be below 55 on this scale and are marked with an icon.

the fitness food categories

 5 a day

 omega-3

 low fat

 low GI

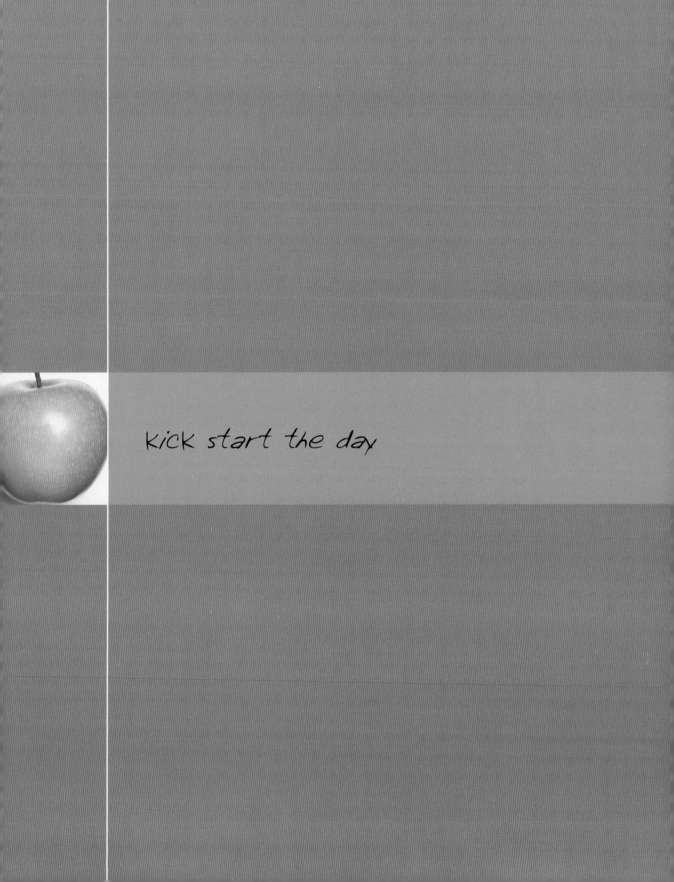

kick start the day

citrus zing

prepare in 10 mins
cooking time 0 mins
serves 4

ingredients
1 pink grapefruit
1 yellow grapefruit
3 oranges

1 Using a sharp knife, carefully cut away all the peel and pith from the grapefruit and oranges.

2 Working over a bowl to catch the juice, carefully cut the grapefruit and orange segments between the membranes to obtain skinless segments of fruit. Discard any pips. Add the segments to the bowl and gently mix together. Cover and let chill until required or divide between 4 serving dishes and serve at once.

Calories 84kcal	Fat 0.24g
Protein 2.4g	Saturates 0.00g
Carbohydrate 19.2g	Fiber 3.78g
Sugar 19.2g	Salt 0.03g

banana breakfast shake

1 Put the bananas, yogurt, skimmed milk, and vanilla extract into a food processor and process until smooth.

2 Serve at once.

prepare in 5 mins
cooking time 0 mins
serves 2

ingredients

2 ripe bananas

$^3/_4$ cup/2 tbsp lowfat yogurt

$^1/_2$ cup skimmed milk

$^1/_2$ tsp vanilla extract

Calories 262kcal	Fat 1.5g
Protein 8.5g	Saturates 0.9g
Carbohydrate 57.1g	Fiber 1.3g
Sugar 34.9g	Salt 0.24g

five a day

prepare in 10 mins
cooking time 0 mins
serves 2

ingredients

24 CARROT
handful of cracked ice
2 carrots, coarsely chopped
4 oz canned pineapple pieces
in juice, drained
3/4 cup pineapple juice, chilled
cucumber slices, to decorate
IN THE PINK
1 blood orange
2-inch piece of cucumber, peeled
and cut into chunks
11/4 cups tomato juice, chilled
dash of Worcestershire sauce
cucumber slices, to decorate
ON THE BEET
6 oz cooked beet, chopped
1/2 cup orange juice, chilled
5 tbsp plain yogurt, chilled
2/3 cup still mineral water, chilled
orange slices, to decorate

1 To make the 24 CARROT, put the ice into the blender, add the carrots, pineapple pieces, and pineapple juice, and process until slushy. Pour into chilled glasses, decorate with cucumber slices, and serve with straws.

2 To make the IN THE PINK, peel the orange, removing all traces of white pith. Holding it over a plate to catch the juice, cut out the segments from the membranes. Squeeze the membranes over the plate to extract any juice. Place the segments and the juice in the blender. Add the cucumber and tomato juice and season to taste with Worcestershire sauce. Process at high speed, then strain into chilled glasses and serve, decorated with cucumber slices.

3 To make the ON THE BEET, put the beet, orange juice, yogurt, and water into the blender. Process until smooth, then pour into chilled glasses, and serve, decorated with orange slices.

Calories 91kcal	Fat 0.33g
Protein 0.9g	Saturates 0.08g
Carbohydrate 22.5g	Fiber 2.21g
Sugar 22.1g	Salt 0.07g

porridge

1 Heat the water in a pan until boiling and pour in the oats, stirring continuously.

2 Let return to a boil and continue to stir for about 5 minutes (or according to the package directions).

3 Add salt or sugar to taste and serve at once in a warm bowl. The nutritional information below is based on no sugar having been added.

prepare in 5 mins
cooking time 10 – 15 mins
serves 1

ingredients

1¹/₄ cups water

¹/₂ cup rolled oats

salt

Calories 160kcal	Fat 3.48g
Protein 5.0g	Saturates 0.00g
Carbohydrate 29.1g	Fiber 2.72g
Sugar 0.0g	Salt 0.09g

exotic dried fruit compote

prepare in 5 mins
cooking time 15 mins
serves 4

ingredients

generous 1/2 cup no-soak dried peaches

1/2 cup no-soak dried apricots

1/2 cup no-soak dried pineapple chunks

2 oz/55 g no-soak dried mango slices

1 cup unsweetened clear apple juice

4 tbsp lowfat plain yogurt (optional)

1 Put the dried fruit into a small pan with the apple juice. Bring slowly to a boil, then reduce the heat to low, cover, and let simmer for 10 minutes.

2 Spoon into serving dishes and top each serving with a tablespoon of yogurt, if desired. Serve at once.

Calories 165kcal	Fat 0.92g
Protein 5.1g	Saturates 0.26g
Carbohydrate 36.6g	Fiber 4.85g
Sugar 36.5g	Salt 0.09g

fresh fruit granola

prepare in 5 mins
cooking time 0 mins
serves 1

ingredients

4 oz/115 g fresh fruit
(e.g. apples, strawberries,
peaches, apricots)
1 tbsp oatmeal flakes, presoaked
1 tbsp water
1 tsp chopped hazelnuts

1 Wash the fresh fruit and trim as necessary. Chop or slice.

2 Mix in the cereal base and water.

3 Sprinkle with chopped hazelnuts.

Calories 129kcal	Fat 4.6g
Protein 3.4g	Saturates 0.2g
Carbohydrate 19.8g	Fiber 4.36g
Sugar 8.8g	Salt 0.02g

bircher granola

1 Put the oats and apple juice into a mixing bowl and combine well. Cover and let chill overnight.

2 To serve, stir the apple and yogurt into the soaked oats and divide between 4 serving bowls. Top with the blackberries and plums.

prepare in 5 mins + 8 hrs soaking
cooking time 0 mins
serves 4

ingredients

scant 1³/₄ cups rolled oats

1 cup apple juice

1 apple, grated

¹/₂ cup plain yogurt

scant ³/₄ cup blackberries

2 plums, pitted and sliced

Calories 217kcal	Fat 3.8g
Protein 6.8g	Saturates 0.2g
Carbohydrate 41.7g	Fiber 4.6g
Sugar 14.4g	Salt 0.09g

yogurt with honey, nuts & blueberries

prepare in 5 mins
cooking time 5 mins +
5 mins cooling
serves 4

ingredients

3 tbsp honey

generous 5/8 cup mixed
unsalted nuts

8 tbsp plain lowfat yogurt

7/8 cup fresh blueberries

1 Heat the honey in a small pan over medium heat, add the nuts and stir until they are well coated. Remove from the heat and let cool slightly.

2 Divide the yogurt between 4 serving bowls, then spoon over the nut mixture and blueberries.

Calories 231kcal	Fat 11.7g
Protein 8.9g	Saturates 2.1g
Carbohydrate 24.1g	Fiber 1.6g
Sugar 1.0g	Salt 0.3g

scrambled eggs with smoked salmon

1 Break the eggs into a large bowl and whisk together with the milk and dill. Season to taste with salt and pepper. Add the smoked salmon and mix to combine.

2 Melt the butter in a large nonstick skillet and pour in the egg and smoked salmon mixture. Using a wooden spatula, gently scrape the egg away from the sides of the skillet as it starts to set and swirl the skillet slightly to allow the uncooked egg to fill the surface.

3 When the eggs are almost cooked but still creamy, remove from the heat and spoon onto the prepared toast, if using. Serve at once, garnished with a sprig of dill.

prepare in 10 mins
cooking time 5 mins
serves 4

ingredients

4 eggs

1/3 cup lowfat milk

2 tbsp chopped fresh dill, plus
    extra for garnishing

salt and pepper

1 1/2 oz/50 g smoked salmon,
    cut into small pieces

2 tbsp butter

slices rustic bread, toasted (optional)

Calories 148kcal	Fat 10.6g
Protein 12.3g	Saturates 4.2g
Carbohydrate 1.1g	Fiber 0.1g
Sugar 1.1g	Salt 1.0g

asparagus with poached eggs & parmesan

prepare in 10 mins
cooking time 10 mins
serves 4

ingredients

10¹/₂ oz/300 g asparagus,
trimmed

4 large eggs

2 oz/60 g Parmesan cheese

pepper

1 Bring 2 pans of water to a boil. Add the asparagus to 1 pan, return to a simmer, and cook for 5 minutes, or until just tender.

2 Meanwhile, reduce the heat of the second pan to a simmer and carefully crack in the eggs, one at a time. Poach for 3 minutes, or until the whites are just set but the yolks are still soft. Remove with a slotted spoon.

3 Drain the asparagus and divide between 4 warmed plates. Top each plate of asparagus with an egg and shave over the cheese. Season to taste with pepper and serve at once.

Calories 169kcal		Fat 11.3g
Protein 15.2g		Saturates 4.6g
Carbohydrate 1.6g		Fiber 1.3g
Sugar 1.5g		Salt 0.48g

tuscan beans on ciabatta toast with fresh herbs

1 Heat the oil in a medium sauté pan and cook the onion over low heat until soft. Add the garlic and cook for an additional 1 minute, then add the lima beans, water, and tomato paste. Bring to a boil, stirring occasionally, and cook for 2 minutes.

2 Add the balsamic vinegar, parsley, and basil and stir to combine. Season to taste with pepper and serve over slices of toasted ciabatta.

prepare in 5 mins
cooking time 10 mins
serves 2

ingredients

1 tbsp olive oil

1 small onion, finely diced

1 garlic clove, crushed

9 oz/250 g canned lima beans,
    drained and rinsed

$1/3$ cup water

1 tbsp tomato paste

1 tsp balsamic vinegar

1 tbsp chopped fresh parsley

1 tbsp torn fresh basil

pepper

TO SERVE

slices ciabatta bread, toasted

Calories 370kcal	Fat 9.2g
Protein 14.9g	Saturates 1.3g
Carbohydrate 60.5g	Fiber 6.8g
Sugar 6.8g	Salt 1.18g

baked eggs with spinach

prepare in 10 mins
cooking time 30 mins
serves 4

ingredients
1 tbsp olive oil
3 shallots, finely chopped
1 lb 2 oz/500 g baby spinach leaves
4 tbsp lowfat milk
freshly grated nutmeg
pepper
4 large eggs
2 tbsp Parmesan cheese,
finely grated
TO SERVE
toasted whole-wheat bread

1 Preheat the oven to 400°F/200°C. Heat the oil in a skillet over medium heat, add the shallots, and cook, stirring frequently, for 4–5 minutes, or until soft. Add the spinach, cover, and cook for 2–3 minutes, or until the spinach has wilted. Remove the lid and cook until all the liquid has evaporated.

2 Add the cream to the spinach and season to taste with nutmeg and pepper. Spread the spinach mixture over the base of a shallow gratin dish and make 4 wells in the mixture with the back of a spoon.

3 Crack an egg into each well and sprinkle over the cheese. Bake in the preheated oven for 12–15 minutes, or until the eggs are set. Serve with whole-wheat toast.

Calories 188kcal	Fat 12.5g
Protein 14.6g	Saturates 3.5g
Carbohydrate 4.5g	Fiber 2.9g
Sugar 3.8g	Salt 0.8g

light & lively lunches

winter warmer red lentil soup

prepare in 15 mins
cooking time 40 mins
serves 6

ingredients

generous 1 cup dried red split
lentils
1 red onion, diced
2 large carrots, sliced
1 celery stalk, sliced
1 parsnip, diced
1 garlic clove, crushed
5 cups vegetable stock
2 tsp paprika
freshly ground black pepper
1 tbsp snipped fresh chives,
to garnish

1 Put the lentils, onion, vegetables, garlic, stock, and paprika into a large pan. Bring to a boil and boil rapidly for 10 minutes. Reduce the heat, cover, and let simmer for 20 minutes, or until the lentils and vegetables are tender.

2 Let the soup cool slightly, then purée in small batches in a food processor or blender. Process until the mixture is smooth.

3 Return the soup to the pan and heat through thoroughly. Season to taste with pepper.

4 To serve, ladle the soup into warmed bowls and swirl in a tablespoonful of mascarpone cheese, if desired. Sprinkle the chives over the soup to garnish and serve at once with crusty bread.

Calories 176kcal	Fat 1.6g
Protein 10.6g	Saturates 0.21g
Carbohydrate 31.7g	Fiber 4.92g
Sugar 7.8g	Salt 0.72g

speedy broccoli soup

1 Cut the broccoli into florets and set aside. Cut the thicker broccoli stalks into $1/2$-inch/1-cm dice and put into a large pan with the leek, celery, garlic, potato, stock, and bay leaf. Bring to a boil, then reduce the heat, cover, and let simmer for 15 minutes

2 Add the broccoli florets to the soup and return to a boil. Reduce the heat, cover, and let simmer for an additional 3–5 minutes, or until the potato and broccoli stalks are tender.

3 Remove from the heat and let the soup cool slightly. Remove and discard the bay leaf. Purée the soup, in small batches, in a food processor or blender until smooth.

4 Return the soup to the pan and heat through thoroughly. Season to taste with pepper. Ladle the soup into warmed bowls and serve at once with crusty bread or toasted croutons.

prepare in 10 mins
cooking time 30 mins
serves 6

ingredients
12 oz/350 g broccoli
1 leek, sliced
1 celery stalk, sliced
1 garlic clove, crushed
12 oz/350 g potato, diced
4 cups vegetable stock
1 bay leaf
freshly ground black pepper
TO SERVE
crusty bread or toasted
    croutons (optional)

Calories 86kcal	Fat 1.3g
Protein 4.9g	Saturates 0.15g
Carbohydrate 14.6g	Fiber 2.89g
Sugar 2.0g	Salt 1.09g

fluffy shrimp omelet

prepare in 10 mins

cooking time 10 mins

serves 2 – 4

ingredients

4 oz/115 g cooked shelled
shrimp, thawed if frozen

4 scallions, chopped

2 oz/55 g zucchini, grated

4 eggs, separated

few dashes of Tabasco sauce,
to taste

3 tbsp milk

pepper

1 tbsp corn or olive oil

1 oz/25 g sharp Cheddar
cheese, grated

1 Pat the shrimp dry with paper towels, then mix with the scallions and zucchini in a bowl and set aside.

2 Using a fork, beat the egg yolks with the Tabasco, milk, and pepper to taste in a separate bowl.

3 Whisk the egg whites in a large bowl until stiff, then gently stir the egg yolk mixture into the egg whites, taking care not to overmix.

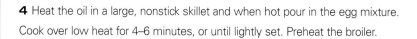

4 Heat the oil in a large, nonstick skillet and when hot pour in the egg mixture. Cook over low heat for 4–6 minutes, or until lightly set. Preheat the broiler.

5 Spoon the shrimp mixture on top of the eggs and sprinkle with the cheese. Cook under the preheated broiler for 2–3 minutes, or until set and the top is golden brown. Cut into wedges and serve at once.

Calories 179kcal	Fat 12.0g
Protein 16.7g	Saturates 3.8g
Carbohydrate 1.1g	Fiber 0.3g
Sugar 1.1g	Salt 1.51g

broccoli & sesame frittata

1 Cook the broccoli in a pan of lightly salted boiling water for 4 minutes. Add the asparagus after 2 minutes. Drain, then plunge into cold water. Drain again and set aside.

2 Heat the oil in a large skillet over low heat, add the onion, garlic, and orange bell pepper and cook, stirring frequently, for 8 minutes, or until the vegetables have softened.

3 Beat the eggs with the water and salt and pepper to taste in a medium-size bowl. Pour into the skillet, add the broccoli and asparagus, and stir gently. Cook over medium heat for 3–4 minutes, drawing the mixture from the edges of the skillet into the center, allowing the uncooked egg to flow to the edges of the skillet. Preheat the broiler.

4 Sprinkle the top of the frittata with the sesame seeds and cheese and cook under the preheated broiler for 3–5 minutes, or until golden and set. Sprinkle with the scallions, cut into wedges, and serve. Serve either warm or cold.

prepare in 10 mins
cooking time 25 mins
serves 2 – 4

ingredients

6 oz/175 g broccoli, broken into
  small florets

salt and pepper

3 oz/85 g asparagus spears,
  diagonally sliced

1 tbsp virgin olive oil

1 onion, cut into small wedges

2–4 garlic cloves, finely chopped

1 large orange bell pepper,
  seeded and chopped

4 eggs

3 tbsp cold water

$\frac{1}{8}$ cup sesame seeds

$\frac{1}{8}$ cup freshly grated Parmesan
  cheese

3 scallions, finely sliced

Calories 221kcal	Fat 14.9g
Protein 14.1g	Saturates 3.69g
Carbohydrate 8.1g	Fiber 3.52g
Sugar 6.5g	Salt 0.31g

chili bean cakes with avocado salsa

prepare in 10 mins +
30 mins chilling
cooking time 10 mins
serves 4

ingredients

¹/₈ cup pine nuts
15 oz/425 g canned mixed beans, drained and rinsed
¹/₂ red onion, finely chopped
1 tbsp tomato paste
¹/₂ fresh red chili, seeded and finely chopped
1 cup fresh brown bread crumbs
1 egg, beaten
1 tbsp finely chopped fresh cilantro
lowfat spray oil
1 lime, cut into quarters, to garnish
TO SERVE
4 toasted whole-wheat bread rolls
SALSA
1 avocado, pitted, peeled, and chopped
3¹/₂ oz/100 g tomatoes, seeded and chopped
2 garlic cloves, crushed
2 tbsp finely chopped fresh cilantro
pepper
juice of ¹/₂ lime

1 Heat a nonstick skillet over medium heat, add the pine nuts, and cook, turning, until just browned. Tip into a bowl and set aside.

2 Put the beans into a large bowl and coarsely mash. Add the onion, tomato paste, chili, pine nuts, and half the bread crumbs and mix well. Add half the egg and the cilantro and mash together, adding a little more egg, if needed, to bind the mixture.

3 Form the mixture into 4 flat cakes. Coat with the remaining bread crumbs, cover, and let chill in the refrigerator for 30 minutes.

4 To make the salsa, mix all the ingredients together in a serving bowl, cover, and let chill in the refrigerator until required.

5 Heat some spray oil in a skillet over medium heat, add the bean cakes, and cook for 4–5 minutes on each side, or until crisp and heated through. Remove from the skillet and drain on paper towels.

6 Serve each bean cake in a toasted whole-wheat roll, if desired, with the salsa, garnished with a lime quarter.

Calories 345kcal	Fat 15.9g
Protein 14.9g	Saturates 2.9g
Carbohydrate 40.5g	Fiber 8.4g
Sugar 7.4g	Salt 1.59g

warm red lentil salad with goat cheese

1 Heat half the olive oil in a large pan over medium heat, add the cumin seeds, garlic, and ginger and cook for 2 minutes, stirring constantly.

2 Stir in the lentils, then add the stock, a ladleful at a time, until it is all absorbed, stirring constantly—this will take about 20 minutes. Remove from the heat and stir in the herbs.

3 Meanwhile, heat the remaining olive oil in a skillet over medium heat, add the onions, and cook, stirring frequently, for 10 minutes, or until soft and lightly browned.

4 Toss the spinach in the hazelnut oil in a bowl, then divide between 4 serving plates.

5 Mash the goat cheese with the yogurt in a small bowl and season to taste with pepper.

6 Divide the lentils between the serving plates and top with the onions and goat cheese mixture. Garnish with lemon quarters and serve with toasted rye bread.

prepare in 15 mins
cooking time 35 mins
serves 4

ingredients

2 tbsp olive oil

2 tsp cumin seeds

2 garlic cloves, crushed

2 tsp grated fresh gingerroot

$1^1/_2$ cups split red lentils

3 cups vegetable stock

2 tbsp chopped fresh mint

2 tbsp chopped fresh cilantro

2 red onions, thinly sliced

$4^3/_8$ cups baby spinach leaves

1 tsp hazelnut oil

$3^1/_2$ oz/100 g soft goat cheese

4 tbsp lowfat strained
   plain yogurt

pepper

1 lemon, cut into quarters,
   to garnish

toasted rye bread

Calories 422kcal	Fat 12.5g
Protein 28.1g	Saturates 5.4g
Carbohydrate 53g	Fiber 5.8g
Sugar 10g	Salt 1.77g

pasta with spiced leek, butternut squash & cherry tomatoes

prepare in 15 mins
cooking time 25 mins
serves 4

ingredients

5¹/₂ oz/150 g baby leeks,
cut into ³/₄-inch (2-cm) slices
6 oz/175 g, peeled weight,
butternut squash, seeded and
cut into
³/₄-inch (2-cm) chunks
1¹/₂ tbsp medium ready-prepared
curry paste
1 tsp canola or vegetable oil
6 oz/175 g cherry tomatoes
9 oz/250 g dried pasta of your
choice
1¹/₄ cups White Sauce
2 tbsp chopped fresh cilantro
leaves

1 Preheat the oven to 400°F/200°C.

2 Bring a large pan of water to a boil, add the leeks, and cook for 2 minutes. Add the butternut squash and cook for an additional 2 minutes. Drain in a colander.

3 Mix the curry paste with the oil in a large bowl. Toss the leeks and butternut squash in the mixture to coat thoroughly.

4 Transfer the leeks and butternut squash to a nonstick baking sheet and roast in the oven for 10 minutes until golden brown. Add the tomatoes and roast for an additional 5 minutes.

5 Meanwhile, cook the pasta according to the instructions on the package and drain.

6 Put the sauce into a large pan and warm over low heat. Add the leeks, butternut squash, tomatoes, and cilantro and stir in the warm pasta. Mix thoroughly and serve.

Calories 291kcal	Fat 3.0g
Protein 11.9g	Saturates 0.5g
Carbohydrate 62.8g	Fiber 4.1g
Sugar 9.5g	Salt 0.25g

cajun chicken salad

1 Make 3 diagonal slashes across each chicken breast. Put the chicken into a shallow dish and sprinkle all over with the Cajun seasoning. Cover and let chill for at least 30 minutes.

2 When ready to cook, brush a stove-top grill pan with the corn oil, if using. Heat over high heat until very hot and a few drops of water sprinkled into the pan sizzle immediately. Add the chicken and cook for 7–8 minutes on each side, or until thoroughly cooked. If still slightly pink in the center, cook a little longer. Remove the chicken and set aside.

3 Add the mango slices to the pan and cook for 2 minutes on each side. Remove and set aside.

4 Meanwhile, arrange the salad greens in a salad bowl and sprinkle over the onion, beet, radishes, and walnut halves.

5 Put the walnut oil, mustard, lemon juice, and salt and pepper to taste in a screw-top jar and shake until well blended. Pour over the salad and sprinkle with the sesame seeds.

6 Arrange the mango and the salad on a serving plate and top with the chicken breast and a few of the salad greens.

prepare in 5 mins +
30 mins chilling

cooking time 15 mins

serves 4

ingredients

4 skinless, boneless chicken
   breasts, about 5 oz/140 g each

4 tsp Cajun seasoning

2 tsp corn oil (optional)

1 ripe mango, peeled, seeded,
   and cut into thick slices

7 oz/200 g mixed salad greens

1 red onion, thinly sliced and cut
   in half

6 oz/175 g cooked beet, diced

3 oz/85 g radishes, sliced

generous 3/8 cup walnut halves

4 tbsp walnut oil

1–2 tsp Dijon mustard

1 tbsp lemon juice

salt and pepper

2 tbsp sesame seeds

Calories 425kcal	Fat 17.24g
Protein 52.3g	Saturates 2.12g
Carbohydrate 14.7g	Fiber 3.74g
Sugar 13.2g	Salt 0.67g

tomato, mozzarella & avocado salad

prepare in 15 mins
cooking time 0 mins
serves 4

ingredients

2 ripe beefsteak tomatoes

3¹/₂ oz/100 g mozzarella
cheese

2 avocados

1 tbsp olive oil

1¹/₂ tbsp white wine vinegar

1 tsp coarse grain mustard

salt and pepper

few fresh basil leaves, torn into
pieces

20 black olives

TO SERVE

fresh crusty bread

1 Using a sharp knife, cut the tomatoes into thick wedges and place in a large serving dish. Drain the mozzarella cheese and coarsely tear into pieces. Cut the avocados in half and remove the pits. Cut the flesh into slices, then arrange the mozzarella cheese and avocado with the tomatoes.

2 Mix the oil, vinegar, and mustard together in a small bowl, add salt and pepper to taste, then drizzle over the salad.

3 Sprinkle the basil and olives over the top and serve at once with fresh crusty bread.

Calories 205kcal	Fat 17.4g
Protein 6.8g	Saturates 5.8g
Carbohydrate 5.5g	Fiber 3.3g
Sugar 5.0g	Salt 1.3g

tomato, salmon & shrimp salad

1 Halve most of the cherry tomatoes. Place the lettuce leaves round the edge of a shallow bowl and add all the tomatoes and cherry tomatoes. Using scissors, snip the smoked salmon into strips and sprinkle over the tomatoes, then add the shrimp.

2 Mix the mustard, sugar, vinegar, and oil together in a small bowl, then tear most of the dill sprigs into it. Mix well and pour over the salad. Toss well to coat the salad with the dressing. Snip the remaining dill over the top and season to taste with pepper.

3 Serve the salad with warmed rolls or ciabatta bread.

prepare in 20 mins
cooking time 0 mins
serves 4

ingredients

4 oz/115 g cherry or baby plum
  tomatoes
several lettuce leaves
4 ripe tomatoes, coarsely
  chopped
3^1/$_2$ oz/100 g smoked salmon
7 oz/200 g large cooked shrimp,
  thawed if frozen
1 tbsp Dijon mustard
2 tsp superfine sugar
2 tsp red wine vinegar
2 tbsp medium olive oil
few fresh dill sprigs
pepper
TO SERVE
warmed rolls or ciabatta bread

Calories 151kcal	Fat 7.4g
Protein 20g	Saturates 1.1g
Carbohydrate 1.2g	Fiber 0.3g
Sugar 1.1g	Salt 1.75g

roasted vegetable salad

prepare in 5 mins
cooking time 40 mins
serves 4

ingredients

1 onion
1 eggplant, about 8 oz/225 g
1 red bell pepper, seeded
1 orange bell pepper, seeded
1 large zucchini, about 6 oz/175 g
2–4 garlic cloves
2–4 tbsp olive oil
salt and pepper
1 tbsp balsamic vinegar
2 tbsp extra-virgin olive oil
1 tbsp shredded fresh basil
TO SERVE
freshly shaved Parmesan cheese

1 Preheat the oven to 400°F/200°C. Cut all the vegetables into even-size wedges, put into a roasting pan, and sprinkle over the garlic. Pour over 2 tablespoons of the olive oil and turn the vegetables in the oil until well coated. Add a little salt and pepper. Roast in the preheated oven for 40 minutes, or until tender, adding the extra olive oil if becoming too dry.

2 Meanwhile, put the vinegar, extra-virgin olive oil, and salt and pepper to taste into a screw-top jar and shake until blended.

3 Once the vegetables are cooked, remove from the oven, arrange on a serving dish, and pour over the dressing. Sprinkle with the basil and serve with shavings of Parmesan cheese. Serve warm or cold.

Calories 190kcal	Fat 15.21g
Protein 3.7g	Saturates 2.59g
Carbohydrate 10.1g	Fiber 3.46g
Sugar 8.5g	Salt 0.06g

three bean salad

1 Arrange the salad greens in a salad bowl and set aside.

2 Thinly slice the onion, then cut in half to form half moons and put into a bowl.

3 Thinly slice the radishes, cut the tomatoes in half, and peel the beet if necessary and dice. Add to the onion with the remaining ingredients, except the nuts and cheese.

4 Put all the ingredients for the dressing into a screw-top jar and shake until blended. Pour over the bean mixture, toss lightly, then spoon on top of the salad greens.

5 Sprinkle over the nuts and cheese and serve at once.

prepare in 5 mins
cooking time 0 mins
serves 4 – 6

ingredients
6 oz/175 g mixed salad greens, such as spinach, arugula, and frisée
1 red onion
3 oz/85 g radishes
6 oz/175 g cherry tomatoes
4 oz/115 g cooked beet
10 oz/280 g canned cannellini beans, drained and rinsed
7 oz/200 g canned red kidney beans, drained and rinsed
$10^1/_2$ oz/300 g canned flageolets, drained and rinsed
scant $^1/_3$ cup dried cranberries
scant $^1/_4$ cup roasted cashews
$2^1/_2$ oz/70 g feta cheese (drained weight), crumbled
DRESSING
3 tbsp extra-virgin olive oil
1 tsp Dijon mustard
2 tbsp lemon juice
1 tbsp chopped fresh cilantro
salt and pepper

Calories 301kcal	Fat 15.9g
Protein 16g	Saturates 5.6g
Carbohydrate 25.2g	Fiber 9.4g
Sugar 7.9g	Salt 1.29g

tabbouleh salad

prepare in 15 mins
cooking time 3 mins +
25 mins soaking
serves 4

ingredients

generous 1 cup bulgur wheat

2 cups boiling water

8 vine-ripened tomatoes, seeded
and chopped

3 inch/7.5 cm piece of cucumber,
diced

3 scallions, finely chopped

4 tbsp chopped fresh mint

4 tbsp chopped fresh cilantro

4 tbsp chopped fresh parsley

8 slices of provolone cheese

DRESSING

juice of $1/2$ lemon

2 tbsp extra-virgin olive oil

salt and pepper

1 Cover the bulgur wheat with the boiling water in a large bowl. Stir and let stand for about 20–25 minutes or until the bulgur is tender but still retains some bite. Drain well.

2 Transfer to a serving bowl and let cool slightly. Add the tomatoes, cucumber, and scallions and toss until combined. Stir in the herbs.

3 Mix together the lemon juice and olive oil to make the dressing and pour it over the salad. Mix well with a spoon, then season with salt and pepper to taste.

4 If serving with the provolone, heat a stovetop grill pan until hot. Place the provolone on the pan and cook for about 2–3 minutes, turning halfway. Serve the provolone on top of the tabbouleh.

Calories 335kcal	Fat 14.58g
Protein 12.3g	Saturates 6.34g
Carbohydrate 39.9g	Fiber 1.94g
Sugar 6.3g	Salt 0.51g

bacon buns

prepare in 10 mins
cooking time 10 mins
serves 4

ingredients

8 low-salt lean smoked Canadian
bacon slices

6 tomatoes

1¹/₈ cups lowfat plain cottage
cheese

freshly ground black pepper

4 large seeded whole-wheat or
white bread rolls

2 scallions, chopped

1 Preheat the broiler to high. Remove any visible fat and rind from the bacon and cut 4 of the tomatoes in half. Place the bacon and tomatoes, cut-side up, under the preheated broiler and cook, turning the bacon over halfway through, for 8–10 minutes, or until the bacon is crisp and the tomatoes are softened. Remove the tomatoes and bacon from the broiler and drain the bacon on paper towels to help remove any excess fat. Keep the bacon and tomatoes warm.

2 Meanwhile, cut the remaining tomatoes into bite-size pieces and combine with the cottage cheese in a bowl. Cut the bacon into bite-size pieces and stir into the cottage cheese mixture. Season to taste with pepper.

3 Cut the bread rolls in half and divide the bacon filling evenly over each roll base. Sprinkle the scallions over the filling and cover with the roll tops. Serve at once with the broiled tomatoes.

Calories 263kcal	Fat 7.3g
Protein 19.8g	Saturates 2.7g
Carbohydrate 31.8g	Fiber 3.8g
Sugar 7.9g	Salt 1.82g

spiced risotto cakes with mango, lime & cream cheese

1 Preheat the oven to 400°F/200°C.

2 Heat a large, nonstick pan over high heat, add the onion and leek, and cook, stirring constantly, for 2–3 minutes, or until softened but not colored.

3 Add the rice and stock, bring to the boil, then continue to boil, stirring constantly, for 2 minutes. Reduce the heat and cook for an additional 15 minutes, stirring every 2–3 minutes.

4 When the rice is nearly cooked and has absorbed all the stock, stir in the zucchini and basil and cook, continuing to stir, over high heat for an additional 5–10 minutes or until the mixture is sticky and dry. Turn out onto a plate and let cool.

5 Meanwhile, to make the filling, mix the cream cheese, mango, lime zest and juice, and cayenne together in a bowl.

6 Divide the cooled rice mixture into 3 and form into cakes. Make an indentation in the center of each cake and fill with 1 tbsp of the filling. Mold the sides up and over to seal in the filling, then reshape with a palette knife. Coat each cake with bread crumbs and arrange on a nonstick baking sheet.

7 Spray each cake lightly with oil and bake in the oven for 15–20 minutes, or until a light golden brown color. Serve with salad greens.

prepare in 30 mins + 30 mins cooling

cooking time 45 – 50 mins

serves 3

ingredients

3 oz/85 g, peeled weight, onion, finely chopped

3 oz/85 g leek, finely chopped

$^1/_8$ cup risotto rice

scant 2$^1/_2$ cups vegetable stock

scant $^1/_2$ cup grated zucchini

1 tbsp fresh basil, chopped

$^1/_2$ cup fresh whole wheat breadcrumbs

vegetable oil spray

FOR THE FILLING

scant $^1/_4$ cup 4% fat cream cheese

1$^3/_4$ oz/50 g, peeled weight, mango, diced

1 tsp finely grated lime zest

1 tsp lime juice

pinch of cayenne pepper

Calories 113kcal	Fat 2.5g
Protein 4.5g	Saturates 0.8g
Carbohydrate 15.3g	Fiber 1.8g
Sugar 4.8g	Salt 0.9g

raisin coleslaw & tuna-filled pita breads

prepare in 5 mins
cooking time 5 mins
serves 4

ingredients

scant $^1/_2$ cup grated carrot

2 oz/55 g white cabbage, thinly
sliced

$^1/_3$ cup lowfat plain yogurt

1 tsp cider vinegar

generous $^1/_8$ cup raisins

7 oz/200 g canned tuna steak in
water, drained

2 tbsp pepitas

freshly ground black pepper

4 whole-wheat or white
pita breads

4 eating apples, to serve

1 Mix the carrot, cabbage, yogurt, vinegar, and raisins together in a bowl. Lightly stir in the tuna and half the pepitas and season to taste with pepper.

2 Lightly toast the pita breads under a preheated hot broiler or in a toaster, then let cool slightly. Using a sharp knife, cut each pita bread in half. Divide the filling evenly between the pita breads and sprinkle the remaining pepitas over the filling. Core and cut the apples into wedges, then serve at once with the filled pita breads.

Calories 353kcal
Protein 22.2g
Carbohydrate 52.9g
Sugar 10.0g

Fat 7.18g
Saturates 1.32g
Fiber 5.25g
Salt 1.00g

desirable dinners

easy gazpacho

prepare in 10 mins +
2 hrs chilling
cooking time 0 mins
serves 4

ingredients

1 small cucumber, peeled
and chopped
2 red bell peppers, seeded
and chopped
2 green bell peppers, seeded
and chopped
2 garlic cloves,
coarsely chopped
1 fresh basil sprig
2¹/₂ cups strained tomatoes
1 tbsp extra-virgin olive oil
1 tbsp red wine vinegar
1 tbsp balsamic vinegar
1¹/₄ cups Vegetable Stock
2 tbsp lemon juice
salt and pepper
TO SERVE
2 tbsp diced, peeled cucumber
2 tbsp finely chopped red onion
2 tbsp finely chopped
red bell pepper
2 tbsp finely chopped
green bell pepper
ice cubes
4 fresh basil sprigs
fresh crusty bread

1 Put the cucumber, bell peppers, garlic, and basil in a food processor and process for 1¹/₂ minutes. Add the strained tomatoes, olive oil, and both kinds of vinegar and process until smooth.

2 Pour in the Vegetable Stock and lemon juice and stir. Transfer the mixture to a large bowl. Season to taste with salt and pepper. Cover with plastic wrap and let chill in the refrigerator for at least 2 hours.

3 To serve, prepare the cucumber, onion, and bell peppers, then place in small serving dishes or arrange decoratively on a plate. Place ice cubes in 4 large soup bowls. Stir the soup and ladle it into the bowls. Garnish with the basil sprigs and serve with the prepared vegetables and chunks of fresh crusty bread.

Calories 128kcal	Fat 3.89g
Protein 4.7g	Saturates 0.57g
Carbohydrate 19.1g	Fiber 5.79g
Sugar 17.4g	Salt 1.61g

rustic roasted ratatouille

1 Preheat the oven to 400°F/200°C.

2 Bake the potatoes in their skins in the oven for 30 minutes, remove, and cut into wedges—the flesh should not be completely cooked.

3 To make the marinade, put all the ingredients into a bowl and blend together with a hand-held electric blender until smooth, or use a food processor.

4 Put the potato wedges into a large bowl with the eggplant, onion, bell peppers, and zucchini, pour over the marinade, and mix thoroughly.

5 Arrange the vegetables on a nonstick baking sheet and roast in the oven, turning occasionally, for 25–30 minutes, or until golden brown and tender. Add the tomatoes for the last 5 minutes of the cooking time just to split the skins and warm slightly.

6 Mix the cream cheese, honey, and paprika together in a bowl.

7 Serve the vegetables with a little of the cream cheese mixture, and sprinkled with chopped parsley.

prepare in 30 mins
cooking time 1 hour
serves 4

ingredients
10¹/₂ oz/300 g potatoes in their skins, scrubbed
7 oz/200 g eggplant, cut into ¹/₂-inch (1-cm) wedges
4¹/₂ oz/125 g, peeled weight, red onion cut into ¹/₄-inch (5-mm) rings
7 oz/200 g seeded mixed bell peppers, sliced into ¹/₂-inch (1-cm) strips
6 oz/175 g zucchini, cut in half lengthwise, then into ¹/₂-inch (1-cm) slices
4¹/₂ oz/125 g cherry tomatoes
scant ¹/₂ cup 0% fat cream cheese
1 tsp honey
pinch of smoked paprika
1 tsp chopped fresh parsley
FOR THE MARINADE
1 tsp canola or vegetable oil
1 tbsp lemon juice
4 tbsp white wine
1 tsp sugar
2 tbsp chopped fresh basil
1 tsp finely chopped fresh rosemary
1 tbsp finely chopped fresh lemon thyme
¹/₄ tsp smoked paprika

Calories 200kcal	Fat 3.0g
Protein 5.8g	Saturates 1g
Carbohydrate 25.9g	Fiber 4.0g
Sugar 12.2g	Salt 0.06g

sweet & sour sea bass

prepare in 25 mins +
30 mins cooling

cooking time 15 mins

serves 2

ingredients

2¼ oz/60 g bok choy, shredded

generous ¼ cup bean sprouts

1½ oz/40 g shiitake
mushrooms, sliced

1½ oz/40 g oyster
mushrooms, torn

¾ oz/20 g scallion, finely sliced

1 tsp finely grated gingerroot

1 tbsp finely sliced lemongrass

2 x 3¼ oz/2 x 90 g sea bass
fillets, skinned and boned

1 tbsp sesame seeds, toasted

FOR THE SWEET & SOUR SAUCE

⅓ cup unsweetened
pineapple juice

1 tbsp sugar

1 tbsp red wine vinegar

2 star anise, crushed

⅓ cup tomato juice

1 tbsp cornstarch, blended with
a little cold water

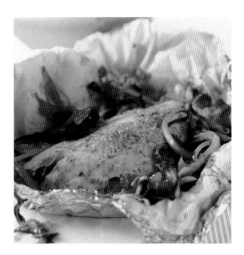

1 Preheat the oven to 400°F/200°C. Cut 2 x 15-inch (38-cm) squares of waxed paper and 2 of the same size aluminum foil squares.

2 To make the sauce, heat the pineapple juice, sugar, red wine vinegar, star anise, and tomato juice in a pan, let simmer for 1–2 minutes then thicken with the cornstarch and water mixture, whisking constantly, then pass through a fine strainer into a small bowl to cool.

3 In a separate large bowl mix together the bok choy, bean sprouts, mushrooms, and scallions, then add the ginger and lemongrass. Toss all the ingredients together.

4 Put a square of waxed paper on top of a square of foil and fold into a triangle. Open up and place half the vegetable mix into the center, pour half the sweet-and-sour sauce over the vegetables and place the sea bass on top. Sprinkle with a few sesame seeds. Close the triangle over the mixture and, starting at the top, fold the right corner and crumple the edges together to form an airtight triangular bag. Repeat to make the second bag.

5 Place onto a baking sheet and cook in the oven for 10 minutes until the foil bags puff with steam. To serve, place on individual plates and snip open at the table so that you can enjoy the wonderful aromas as the bag is opened.

Calories 150kcal	Fat 3.0g
Protein 20.5g	Saturates 0.5g
Carbohydrate 28.0g	Fiber 1.5g
Sugar 15.8g	Salt 0.05g

fresh baked sardines

1 Slice 1 of the lemons and grate and squeeze the juice from the second one.

2 Cut the heads off the sardines and place the fish in a shallow, ovenproof dish, large enough to hold them in a single layer. Place the lemon slices between the fish. Drizzle the lemon juice and oil over the fish. Sprinkle over the lemon rind and oregano and season with salt and pepper.

3 Bake in a preheated oven, 375°F/190°C, for 20–30 minutes, until the fish are tender. Serve garnished with lemon wedges.

prepare in 10 mins
cooking time 30 mins
serves 4

ingredients
2 lemons
12 large fresh sardines, gutted
2 tbsp olive oil
4 tbsp chopped fresh oregano
salt and pepper
lemon wedges, to garnish

Calories 352kcal	Fat 22.1g
Protein 37.3g	Saturates 5.7g
Carbohydrate 1.1g	Fiber 0.1g
Sugar 0.8g	Salt 0.55g

potato, herb & smoked salmon gratin

prepare in 25 mins +
20 mins cooling

cooking time 50 mins

serves 6

ingredients

1³/₄ cups lowfat milk

3 whole cloves

2 bay leaves

1³/₄ oz/50 g, peeled weight,
onion, sliced

3 oz/85 g leek, chopped

3¹/₂ oz/100 g lightly cured smoked
salmon, finely sliced into strips

12 oz/350 g, peeled weight,
potatoes, cut into

¹/₁₆-inch (2-mm) slices

2 tbsp finely chopped fresh chives

2 tbsp finely chopped fresh dill

1 tbsp finely chopped fresh tarragon

2 tsp whole grain mustard

pepper, to taste

1¹/₄ oz/35 g watercress

1 Preheat the oven to 400°F/200°C. Line the bottom of a 7¹/₂-inch (19-cm) sandwich pan with waxed paper.

2 Pour the milk into a large, heavy-bottom pan, add the cloves, bay leaves, onion, leek, and smoked salmon and heat over a low heat.

3 When the milk is just about to reach simmering point, carefully remove the smoked salmon with a slotted spoon and let cool on a plate.

4 Add the potatoes to the milk and stir with a wooden spoon. Return to a simmer and cook, stirring occasionally to prevent the potatoes from sticking, for 12 minutes, or until the potatoes are just beginning to soften and the milk has thickened slightly from the potato starch. Remove the cloves and bay leaves.

5 Add the herbs, mustard, and pepper and stir well. Pour the mixture into the prepared pan. Cover with a layer of waxed paper and then foil and bake in the oven for 30 minutes.

6 Remove from the oven and place a pan on top. Let cool for 20 minutes before turning out onto a baking sheet. Put under a preheated hot broiler to brown the top. Cut the gratin into 6 wedges and serve with the smoked salmon, tossed with the watercress.

Calories 107kcal	Fat 2.0g
Protein 8.5g	Saturates 0.8g
Carbohydrate 14.5g	Fiber 1.4g
Sugar 4.4g	Salt 0.9g

chili chicken with chickpea mash

1 Make shallow cuts in each chicken breast. Place the chicken in a dish, brush with the olive oil, and coat both sides of each breast with the harissa paste. Season well with salt and pepper, cover the dish with foil, and let marinate in the refrigeratorfor 30 minutes.

2 Preheat the oven to 425°F/220°C. Transfer the chicken breasts to a roasting pan and roast for about 20–30 minutes until they are cooked through and there is no trace of pink in the center.

3 Meanwhile make the chickpea mash. Heat the oil in a pan and gently fry the garlic for 1 minute, then add the chickpeas and milk and heat through for a few minutes. Transfer to a blender or food processor and purée until smooth. Season to taste with salt and pepper and stir in the fresh cilantro.

4 To serve, divide the chickpea mash between 4 serving plates, top each one with a chicken breast, and garnish with cilantro.

prepare in 15 mins +
30 mins marinating
cooking time 30 mins
serves 4

ingredients

4 skinless chicken breasts, about
   5 oz/140 g each

1 tbsp olive oil

8 tsp harissa (chili) paste

salt and black pepper

CHICKPEA MASH

2 tbsp olive oil

2–3 garlic cloves, crushed

14 oz/400 g no salt or sugar
   canned chickpeas,
   drained and rinsed

4 tbsp semiskim milk

3 tbsp chopped fresh cilantro

Calories 321kcal	Fat 12.93g
Protein 36.8g	Saturates 2.09g
Carbohydrate 15.3g	Fiber 0.06g
Sugar 1.5g	Salt 1.04g

roasted squash wedges
with risotto & asparagus

prepare in 20
cooking time 25 mins
serves 4

ingredients

1 x 7 oz/200 g acorn squash or
other type of squash, peeled,
seeded, and cut into 4 wedges
1 tsp canola or vegetable oil
3¹/₂ oz/100 g, peeled weight,
onion, finely chopped
1 tsp crushed garlic
2¹/₂ oz/70 g three-grain risotto
mix (baldo rice, spelt, and pearl
barley—this is available
ready-mixed)
2¹/₂ cups vegetable stock
8¹/₄ oz/235 g asparagus tips
2 tbsp finely chopped fresh
marjoram, plus extra to garnish
3 tbsp 0% fat cream cheese
2 tbsp finely chopped
fresh parsley
pepper, to taste

1 Preheat the oven to 400°F/200°C. Spread out the squash wedges on a nonstick baking sheet and roast in the oven for 20 minutes, or until tender and golden brown.

2 Meanwhile, heat the oil in a medium pan over high heat, add the onion and garlic, and cook, stirring, until softened but not colored. Add the risotto mix and stir in half the stock. Simmer, stirring occasionally, until the stock has reduced in the pan. Pour in the remaining stock and continue to cook, stirring occasionally, until the grains are tender.

3 Cut 6 oz (175 g) of the asparagus into 4-inch (10-cm) lengths and blanch in a pan of boiling water for 2 minutes. Drain and keep warm. Cut the remaining asparagus into ¹/₄-inch (5-mm) slices and add to the risotto for the last 3 minutes of the cooking time.

4 Remove the risotto from the heat and stir in the marjoram, cream cheese, and parsley. Season with pepper. Do not reboil.

5 To serve, lay the squash wedges on warmed serving plates, then spoon over the risotto and top with the asparagus. Garnish with marjoram.

Calories 121kcal	Fat 1.5g
Protein 7.5g	Saturates 1.68g
Carbohydrate 23.9g	Fiber 2.6g
Sugar 5.8g	Salt 1.73g

turkey with sun-dried tomato tapenade

1 Place the turkey steaks in a shallow, nonmetallic dish. Mix all the marinade ingredients together in a pitcher, whisking well to mix. Pour the marinade over the turkey steaks, turning to coat. Cover with plastic wrap and let marinate in the refrigerator for at least 1 hour.

2 To make the tapenade, put all the ingredients into a food processor and process to a smooth paste. Transfer to a bowl, then cover with plastic wrap and let chill in the refrigerator until required.

3 Drain the turkey steaks, reserving the marinade. Then heat the grill pan and cook over medium–high heat for 10–15 minutes, turning and brushing frequently with the reserved marinade. Transfer the turkey steaks to 4 large serving plates and top with the sun-dried tomato tapenade. Serve immediately.

prepare in 5 mins +
1 hr marinating
cooking time 15 mins
serves 4

ingredients
4 turkey steaks
MARINADE
$^2/_3$ cup white wine
1 tbsp white wine vinegar
1 tbsp olive oil
1 garlic clove, crushed
1 tbsp chopped fresh parsley
pepper
TAPENADE
$1^2/_3$ cups sun-dried tomatoes
  in oil, drained and rinsed
4 canned anchovy fillets,
  drained and rinsed
1 garlic clove, crushed
1 tablespoon lemon juice
3 tablespoons chopped
  fresh parsley

Calories 366kcal	Fat 24.1g
Protein 27.7g	Saturates 3.5g
Carbohydrate 3.6g	Fiber 2.2g
Sugar 2.4g	Salt 1.46g

lentil bolognese

prepare in 25 mins
cooking time 20 - 25 mins
serves 4

ingredients

1 tsp canola or vegetable oil
1 tsp crushed garlic
1 oz/25 g, peeled weight, onion, finely chopped
1 oz/25 g leek, finely chopped
1 oz/25 g celery, finely chopped
1 oz/25 g seeded green bell pepper, finely chopped
1 oz/25 g, peeled weight, carrot, finely chopped
1 oz/25 g zucchini, finely chopped
3 oz/85 g flat mushrooms, diced
4 tbsp red wine
pinch of dried thyme
14 oz/400 g canned tomatoes, chopped, strained through a colander, and the juice and pulp reserved separately
4 tbsp dried Puy (French green) lentils, cooked
pepper, to taste
2 tsp lemon juice
1 tsp sugar
3 tbsp chopped fresh basil, plus extra sprigs to garnish
5 oz/140 g dried spaghetti

1 Heat a pan over low heat, add the oil and garlic, and cook, stirring, until golden brown. Add all the vegetables, except the mushrooms, increase the heat to medium, and cook, stirring occasionally, for 10–12 minutes, or until softened and there is no liquid from the vegetables left in the pan. Add the mushrooms.

2 Increase the heat to high, add the wine, and cook for 2 minutes. Add the thyme and juice from the tomatoes and cook until reduced by half.

3 Add the lentils and pepper, stir in the tomatoes, and cook for an additional 3–4 minutes.

4 Meanwhile, cook the spaghetti according to the instructions on the package.

5 Remove the pan from the heat and stir in the lemon juice, sugar, and basil.

6 Serve the sauce with the cooked spaghetti, garnished with basil sprigs.

Calories 210kcal	Fat 2.0g
Protein 11.0g	Saturates 1.23g
Carbohydrate 42g	Fiber 4.4g
Sugar 6.9g	Salt 0.02g

roast beef salad

prepare in 10 – 15 mins
cooking time 45 – 50 mins
serves 4

ingredients

21 oz/600 g beef fillet, trimmed
of any visible fat
pepper
2 tsp Worcestershire sauce
2 tbsp olive oil
14 oz/400 g green beans
3¹/₂ oz/100 g small pasta,
such as orecchiette
2 red onions, finely sliced
1 large head radicchio
generous ¹/₄ cup
green olives, pitted
DRESSING
1 tsp Dijon mustard
2 tbsp white wine vinegar
3 tbsp olive oil

1 Preheat the oven to 425°F/220°C. Rub the beef with pepper to taste and Worcestershire sauce. Heat 2 tablespoons of the oil in a small roasting pan over high heat, add the beef, and sear on all sides. Transfer the dish to the preheated oven and roast for 30 minutes. Remove and let cool.

2 Bring a large pan of water to a boil, add the beans, and cook for 5 minutes, or until just tender. Remove with a slotted spoon and refresh the beans under cold running water. Drain and put into a large bowl.

3 Return the bean cooking water to a boil, add the pasta, and cook for 11 minutes, or until tender. Drain and return to the saucepan.

4 Add the pasta to the beans with the onions, radicchio leaves and olives in a serving dish or salad bowl and arrange some thinly sliced beef on top.

5 Whisk the dressing ingredients together in a separate bowl, then pour over the salad and serve at once with extra sliced beef.

Calories 471kcal	Fat 23.1g
Protein 38.4g	Saturates 6.2g
Carbohydrate 29.2g	Fiber 5.0g
Sugar 8.0g	Salt 1.1g

blackened snapper with
sweetcorn papaya relish

1 To make the relish, place the onion, sugar, vinegar, corn, chili, water, mustard seeds, and turmeric into a small pan over medium heat and bring to a boil. Let simmer for 10 minutes, then add the cornstarch mixture, stirring constantly, and cook until it is the required consistency (it will thicken slightly when cooled). Stir in the papaya and let cool.

2 To make the seasoning mix, put all the ingredients into a small bowl and mix thoroughly.

3 Sprinkle the seasoning mix over the snapper fillets on both sides and pat into the flesh, then shake off any excess. Lay the fillets on a cutting board.

4 Heat a nonstick skillet over high heat until smoking. Lightly spray both sides of the fillets with oil, then put into the hot pan and cook for 2 minutes. Turn the fillets and cook all the way through. (If the fillets are thick, finish the cooking under a preheated broiler as the less intense heat will prevent the seasoning mix from burning.) Remove the fish from the skillet.

5 Add the lemon halves, cut-side down, and cook over high heat for 2–5 minutes until browned. Serve the fillets, topped with relish, on warmed plates, with the lemon halves.

prepare in 20 mins + 45 minutes cooling

cooking time 20 minutes

serves 4

ingredients

4 x 3 oz/85 g snapper fillets

vegetable oil spray

2 lemons, halved, to serve

FOR THE RELISH

2 tbsp finely chopped onion

1 tsp sugar

2 tbsp white wine vinegar

2 tbsp cooked or canned corn kernels

1/4 tsp finely chopped habanero chili or other type of chili

generous 1/3 cup water

1/4 tsp yellow mustard seeds

pinch of ground turmeric

1 tsp cornstarch, blended with a little cold water

3/4 oz/50 g papaya, cut into 1/4-inch (5-mm) cubes

FOR THE SEASONING MIX

1/4 tsp paprika

1/2 tsp onion powder

1/4 tsp dried thyme

1/4 tsp dried oregano

1/4 tsp cayenne pepper

1/4 tsp ground black pepper

1/2 tsp cornstarch

Calories 134kcal	Fat 1.7g
Protein 17.4g	Saturates 0.3g
Carbohydrate 13.3g	Fiber 0.3g
Sugar 5.9g	Salt 0.28g

broiled tuna & vegetable kabobs

prepare in 10 mins
cooking time 15 mins
serves 4

ingredients

4 tuna steaks, about
5 oz/140 g each

2 red onions

12 cherry tomatoes

1 red bell pepper, seeded and
diced into 1-inch/2.5-cm pieces

1 yellow bell pepper, seeded and
diced into 1-inch/2.5-cm pieces

1 zucchini, sliced

1 tbsp chopped fresh oregano

4 tbsp olive oil

freshly ground black pepper

lime wedges

selection of salads

TO SERVE

cooked couscous, new potatoes,
or bread

1 Preheat the broiler to high. Cut the tuna into 1-inch/2.5-cm dice. Peel the onions, leaving the root intact, and cut each onion lengthwise into 6 wedges.

2 Divide the fish and vegetables evenly between 8 wooden skewers (presoaked to avoid burning) and arrange on the broiler pan.

3 Mix the oregano and oil together in a small bowl. Season to taste with pepper. Lightly brush the kabobs with the oil and cook under the preheated broiler for 10–15 minutes or until evenly cooked, turning occasionally. If you cannot fit all the kabobs on the broiler pan at once, cook them in batches, keeping the cooked kabobs warm while cooking the remainder. Alternatively, these kabobs can be cooked on a barbecue.

4 Garnish with lime wedges and serve with a selection of salads, cooked couscous, new potatoes, or bread.

Calories 352kcal	Fat 18.10g
Protein 35.8g	Saturates 3.36g
Carbohydrate 12.4g	Fiber 3.05g
Sugar 10.5g	Salt 0.20g

duck breast with noodles &
crunchy rice topping

1 Preheat the oven to 400°F/200°C.

2 Put the orange juice, water, garlic, ginger, spices, orange zest, and sugar into a small pan and bring to a boil. Reduce the heat and simmer for 3–4 minutes.

3 Lay the duck in a small, ovenproof dish and pour over the orange mixture. Cover with a tight-fitting lid or foil and cook in the oven for 1 hour.

4 Soak the rice in cold water for 10 minutes, drain, and pat dry with paper towels. Heat a small, nonstick skillet over medium heat, add the rice, and dry-fry until golden brown. Remove from the heat, tip onto one half of a clean dish towel, then fold the other half over the rice. Using a rolling pin, crush into fine grains.

5 Remove the duck from the cooking liquid with a slotted spoon, shred, and keep warm. Transfer the cooking liquid to a pan over medium heat. Gradually add the cornstarch mixture, stirring constantly, and cook until thickened. Pass through a strainer into a bowl and keep warm.

6 Heat a wok over high heat, then add the oil. Add the vegetables and stir-fry for a few minutes until cooked. Add the noodles, duck, and sauce and briefly stir-fry. Serve in warmed bowls, garnished with scallion and cilantro and sprinkled with the rice.

prepare in 35 mins +
10 mins soaking
cooking time 1 hours
serves 4

ingredients
generous ¹/₄ cup freshly squeezed
  orange juice
generous ¹/₃ cup water
2 tsp crushed garlic
1 tsp finely chopped gingerroot
2 star anise
¹/₄ tsp Szechuan pepper
2 tsp grated orange zest
1 tsp sugar
2 duck breasts, skin and any
  visible fat removed
¹/₈ cup, dry weight, white rice
¹/₂ tsp cornstarch, blended with a
  little cold water
¹/₂ tsp sesame oil
3¹/₂ oz/100 g Napa cabbage,
  shredded
generous 1 cup bean sprouts
5¹/₂ oz/150 g seeded mixed bell
  peppers, finely sliced into strips
1 oz/25 g scallion, finely sliced
  into strips
8³/₄ oz/240 g dry weight, egg
  noodles, refreshed in cold
  water and drained
FOR THE GARNISH
4 tbsp scallion, shredded
4 tbsp chopped fresh
  cilantro leaves

Calories 388kcal	Fat 10.5g
Protein 22g	Saturates 3.1g
Carbohydrate 54.6g	Fiber 2.8g
Sugar 7.4g	Salt 0.42g

monkfish & asparagus stir-fry

prepare in 15 mins
cooking time 15 mins
serves 4

ingredients

1 lb 2 oz/500 g monkfish

4 tbsp vegetable oil

2 zucchini, trimmed, halved,
and sliced

1 red bell pepper,
seeded and sliced

2 garlic cloves, finely chopped

5¹⁄₂ oz/150 g fresh
asparagus spears

3¹⁄₂ oz/100 g snow peas

6 tbsp plain flour

4 tbsp lemon sauce (available
ready-made from supermarkets
and Asian grocery stores)

1 tbsp freshly grated lemongrass

1 tbsp grated fresh gingerroot

salt and pepper

1 Remove any membrane from the monkfish, then cut the flesh into thin slices. Cover the fish with plastic wrap and set aside. Heat 2 tablespoons of the oil in a wok or large skillet, until hot. Add the zucchini and stir-fry for 2 minutes. Add the bell pepper and garlic and cook for another 2 minutes. Add the asparagus and cook for 1 minute, then add the snow peas and cook for 2 minutes. Transfer the vegetables onto a plate.

2 Put the flour in a shallow dish and turn the fish slices in the flour until coated. Heat the remaining oil in the wok or skillet. Add the fish and stir-fry for 5 minutes, or until cooked to your taste (you may need to do this in batches). Transfer the fish to another plate. Put the lemon sauce, lemongrass, and ginger in the wok or skillet.

3 Add the fish and stir-fry over medium heat for a few seconds. Add the vegetables and stir-fry for 1 minute. Season, stir again, and remove from the heat. Transfer to warm plates and serve.

Calories 253kcal	Fat 12.16g
Protein 23.1g	Saturates 1.54g
Carbohydrate 13.6g	Fiber 2.38g
Sugar 12.8g	Salt 0.07g

tuna & avocado salad

1 Toss the avocado, tomatoes, red bell peppers, parsley, garlic, chili and lemon juice together in a large bowl. Season to taste with pepper, cover, and let chill in the refrigerator for 30 minutes.

2 Lightly crush the sesame seeds in a mortar with a pestle. Tip the crushed seeds onto a plate and spread out. Press each tuna steak in turn into the crushed seeds to coat on both sides.

3 Heat the spray oil in a skillet, add the potatoes, and cook, stirring frequently, for 5–8 minutes, or until crisp and brown. Remove from the skillet and drain on paper towels.

4 Wipe out the skillet, add the remaining oil, and heat over high heat until very hot. Add the tuna steaks and cook for 3–4 minutes on each side.

5 To serve, divide the avocado salad between 4 serving plates. Top each with a tuna steak, then sprinkle over the potatoes and a handful of arugula leaves.

prepare in 10 mins + 30 mins chilling

cooking time 20 mins

serves 4

ingredients

1 avocado, pitted, peeled, and cubed

9 oz/250 g cherry tomatoes, halved

2 red bell peppers, seeded and chopped

1 bunch fresh flat-leaf parsley, chopped

2 garlic cloves, crushed

1 fresh red chili, seeded and finely chopped

juice of $^1/_2$ lemon

low-fat spray oil

pepper

3 tbsp sesame seeds

4 fresh tuna steaks, about $5^1/_2$ oz/150 g each

8 cooked new potatoes, cubed

arugula leaves, to serve

Calories 463kcal	Fat 24.1g
Protein 40.2g	Saturates 4.8g
Carbohydrate 22.7g	Fiber 4.9g
Sugar 8.3g	Salt 0.28g

salmon fillet with concassé tomatoes

prepare in 30 mins
cooking time 30 - 35 mins
serves 4

ingredients

4 salmon fillets, about
6 oz/175 g each, trimmed
1 tbsp olive oil
pepper
4 oz/115 g 2 bunches asparagus
spears, trimmed
6 tomatoes, peeled, seeded,
and chopped
1 tbsp chopped fresh dill
grated rind of 1 lemon

1 Preheat the oven to 375°F/190°C. Place the fillets on a cutting board and drizzle with a little oil. Season to taste with pepper. Heat a skillet and cook the fish, nonskin-side down first, until browned. Turn over to brown the other side. Transfer the fish to a roasting pan and cook in the oven for 10–12 minutes, until the fish flakes easily. Melt the butter in a small pan, then let stand until separated. Pour off the clear, clarified butter into a separate pan, and discard the white salty residue.

2 Cook the asparagus for 2–3 minutes in boiling water. Drain, rinse under cold running water, drain again, and set aside.

3 Add the tomatoes, dill and lemon rind to a bowl rind and mix. Divide the asparagus and salmon between 4 plates, spoon some of the tomato dressing over each one, and serve.

Calories 380kcal	Fat 22.8g
Protein 38.5g	Saturates 3.9g
Carbohydrate 5.5g	Fiber 2.6g
Sugar 5.4g	Salt 0.23g

corn & green bean-filled
baked sweet potatoes

1 Preheat the oven to 375°F/190°C. Scrub the sweet potatoes and pierce the skin of each potato with a sharp knife several times. Arrange on a baking sheet and bake in the preheated oven for 1–1¼ hours, or until soft and tender when pierced with the point of a sharp knife. Keep warm.

2 When the potatoes are cooked, bring a pan of water to a boil, add the fava beans and corn, and return to a boil. Reduce the heat, cover, and let simmer for 5 minutes. Trim the green beans, cut in half, and add to the pan. Return to a boil, then reduce the heat, cover, and let simmer for 3 minutes, or until the green beans are just tender.

3 Blend the oil with the vinegar in a small bowl and season to taste with pepper. Drain the corn and beans, return to the pan, add the tomatoes, and pour the dressing over. Add the torn basil leaves and mix well.

4 Remove the sweet potatoes from the oven, cut in half lengthwise, and open up. Divide the corn and bean filling between the potatoes and serve at once, garnished with basil leaves.

prepare in 10 mins
cooking time 1 hr 25 mins
serves 4

ingredients

4 red-fleshed sweet potatoes, about 9 oz/250 g each
1 cup frozen fava beans
scant ¾ cup frozen corn kernels
4 oz/115 g fine long green beans
5 oz/140 g fresh tomatoes, chopped
1 tbsp olive oil
1 tbsp balsamic vinegar
freshly ground black pepper
2 tbsp torn fresh basil leaves, plus extra leaves to garnish

Calories 360kcal	Fat 5.81g
Protein 11.2g	Saturates 1.04g
Carbohydrate 70.3g	Fiber 14.67g
Sugar 22.7g	Salt 0.26g

stuffed vegetables

prepare in 10 mins
cooking time 25 mins
serves 2 – 4

ingredients

2 medium eggplants.

2 tbsp vegetable stock

1 small onion, chopped

2 garlic cloves, crushed

1 tbsp tomato paste

6 ripe tomatoes, skinned
and chopped

4 tbsp cooked brown rice

$^{1}/_{4}$ cup pine nuts, lightly toasted

1 tbsp chopped fresh parsley

1 tbsp chopped fresh mint

1 tbsp chopped fresh basil

$^{1}/_{4}$ tsp ground cinnamon

juice of 1 lemon

black pepper

1 Preheat the oven to 350°Fz(180°C).If stuffing eggplants or zucchini, trim the stems, then halve lengthwise. Use a teaspoon to hollow out each half, leaving a shell about $^{1}/_{2}$ in (1 cm) thick. Chop the scooped-out flesh. Steam the shells over boiling water for about 4 minutes, then hold them under cold water to stop further cooking and dry with paper towels. Mist the insides with oil-and-water spray. If stuffing bell peppers, slice off the tops (put to one side), then scoop out and discard the seeds. If stuffing tomatoes, slice off the tops (put to one side), then scoop out the seeds and flesh, and add the flesh to the rice mixture in step 2.

2 Heat the stock in a skillet, then add the onions and garlic and sauté, stirring, until translucent. Stir in the tomato paste, tomatoes, chopped eggplant or zucchini flesh (if using), cooked rice, pine nuts, herbs, and cinnamon and continue cooking for a couple of minutes.

3 Stir in the lemon juice and season with pepper. Lightly mist a baking dish with oil-and-water spray. Stuff the vegetables with the rice mixture and put the lids back on the peppers or tomatoes. Bake for about 20 minutes

Calories 189kcal		Fat 6.07g	
Protein 5.5g		Saturates 0.74g	
Carbohydrate 30.2g		Fiber 5.33g	
Sugar 9.3g		Salt 0.13g	

ratatouille

1 Heat the oil in a large flameproof casserole over medium heat. Add the onions and stir for 3 minutes. Add the garlic and stir for an additional 3 minutes, or until the onions are soft, but not brown.

2 Stir in the eggplants, zucchini, tomatoes, bouquet garni, sugar, and salt and pepper to taste. Reduce the heat to low, then cover the casserole tightly and simmer for 45 minutes without lifting the lid for at least the first 15 minutes.

3 Taste, and adjust the seasoning if necessary. Sprinkle with the basil leaves and serve immediately or let cool.

prepare in 5 mins
cooking time
50 - 55 mins
serves 4 - 6

ingredients

5 tbsp olive oil

2 large onions, thinly sliced

4 large garlic cloves,
    finely chopped

12 oz/350 g eggplants,
    coarsely chopped

12 oz/350 g zucchini, sliced

4 large beefsteak tomatoes,
    peeled, deseeded,
    and chopped

1 large bouquet garni of 2 large
    sprigs of fresh flat-leaf parsley,
    2 sprigs of fresh thyme, and
    2 sprigs of fresh basil, tied to a
    piece of celery

$1/2$ tsp sugar

salt and pepper

fresh basil leaves, to garnish

Calories 155kcal	Fat 10.20g
Protein 3.6g	Saturates 1.56g
Carbohydrate 13.2g	Fiber 4.25g
Sugar 10.9g	Salt 0.04g

tofu & vegetable stir-fry

prepare in 5 mins
cooking time 10 mins
serves 4

ingredients

2 tbsp vegetable stock
4 scallions, chopped
2 garlic cloves, crushed
1-inch (2.5-cm) piece
fresh gingerroot,
peeled and grated
1/2 fresh red chili, seeded and
finely chopped
1 red and 1 yellow bell pepper,
seeded and sliced
1 cup green beans cut into 1-inch
(2.5-cm) pieces
1 head broccoli,
divided into florets
1 1/3 cups bean sprouts, rinsed
8 oz/225 g firm tofu, cubed
2 tbsp water
juice of 1 lemon
2 tsp sesame oil
1/3 cup blanched almonds, halved

1 Heat the vegetable stock in a wok and stir-fry the scallions, garlic, ginger, and chili for 2 minutes.

2 Add the vegetables and stir-fry for 3–4 minutes. Add the tofu and cook for a further 2 minutes.

3 Mix the water and lemon juice together, then pour over the vegetables and cook for 1 minute.

4 Stir in the sesame oil and almonds and serve immediately on a bed of rice or rice noodles.

Calories 215kcal   Fat 12.91g

Protein 13.9g   Saturates 1.39g

Carbohydrate 11.4g   Fiber 5.92g

Sugar 9.1g   Salt 0.10g

chinese vegetables
& beansprouts with noodles

1 Bring the stock, garlic, and ginger to a boil in a large pan. Stir in the noodles, red bell pepper, peas, broccoli, and mushrooms and return to a boil. Reduce the heat, cover, and let simmer for 5–6 minutes, or until the noodles are tender.

2 Meanwhile, preheat the broiler to medium. Spread the sesame seeds out in a single layer on a baking sheet and toast under the preheated broiler, turning to brown evenly—watch constantly because they brown very quickly. Tip the sesame seeds into a small dish and set aside.

3 Once the noodles are tender, add the water chestnuts, bamboo shoots, Napa cabbage, bean sprouts, and scallions to the pan. Return the stock to a boil, stir to mix the ingredients, and let simmer for an additional 2–3 minutes to heat through thoroughly.

4 Carefully drain off 1¼ cups of the stock into a small heatproof pitcher and set aside. Drain and discard any remaining stock and turn the noodles and vegetables into a warmed serving dish. Quickly mix the soy sauce with the reserved stock and pour over the noodles and vegetables. Season to taste with pepper and serve at once.

prepare in 10 mins
cooking time 20 mins
serves 4

ingredients
5 cups vegetable stock
1 garlic clove, crushed
½-inch/1-cm piece fresh
  gingerroot, finely chopped
8 oz/225 g dried medium
  egg noodles
1 red bell pepper,
  seeded and sliced
¾ cup frozen peas
4 oz/115 g broccoli florets
3 oz/85 g shiitake
  mushrooms, sliced
2 tbsp sesame seeds
8 oz/225 g canned water
  chestnuts, drained and halved
8 oz/225 g canned bamboo
  shoots, drained
10 oz/280 g Napa cabbage, sliced
scant 1 cup bean sprouts
3 scallions, sliced
1 tbsp dark soy sauce
freshly ground black pepper

Calories 353kcal	Fat 9.8g
Protein 14.7g	Saturates 2.04g
Carbohydrate 54.6g	Fiber 6.57g
Sugar 7.9g	Salt 2.34g

apple & plum crumble

prepare in 15 mins
cooking time 35 mins
serves 4

ingredients

4 apples, peeled, cored,
and diced

5 plums, halved, pitted,
and quartered

4 tbsp fresh apple juice

2 tbsp brown sugar

TOPPING

generous 3/4 cup flour

2 3/4 oz/75 g margarine, diced

generous 1/4 cup
buckwheat flakes

generous 1/4 cup rice flakes

1/8 cup sunflower seeds

1/4 cup brown sugar

1/4 tsp ground cinnamon

1 Preheat the oven to 350°F/180°C. Mix the apples, plums, apple juice, and sugar together in a 9-inch/23-cm round pie dish.

2 To make the topping, sift the flour into a mixing bowl and rub in the margarine with your fingertips until it resembles coarse bread crumbs. Stir in the buckwheat and rice flakes, sunflower seeds, sugar, and cinnamon, then spoon the topping over the fruit in the dish.

3 Bake the crumble in the preheated oven for 30–35 minutes, or until the topping is lightly browned and crisp.

Calories 480kcal	Fat 19.0g
Protein 3.4g	Saturates 7.81g
Carbohydrate 79.2g	Fiber 4.42g
Sugar 41.4g	Salt 0.35g

mango cheesecakes

1 Line the bottom and sides of 4 x $^2/_3$-cup ramekins with waxed paper and very lightly oil.

2 Melt the spread in a small pan over low heat, remove from the heat, and stir in the ginger and oats. Mix thoroughly and let cool.

3 Using a sharp knife, cut the mango lengthwise down either side of the thin central seed. Peel the flesh. Cut away any flesh from around the seed and peel. Cut the flesh into chunks and set aside 4 oz/115 g. Put the remaining mango flesh into a food processor or blender and process until smooth. Transfer to a small bowl.

4 Drain away any excess fluid from the cheeses and, using a fork or tablespoon, blend together in a bowl. Finely chop the reserved mango flesh and stir into the cheese mixture along with 1 tablespoon of the mango purée. Divide the cheesecake filling evenly between the ramekins and level with the back of a spoon. Cover each cheesecake evenly with the cooled oat mixture and let chill in the refrigerator for at least 3 hours for the filling to firm. Cover and let chill the mango purée.

5 To serve, carefully trim the lining paper level with the oat mixture. Since the oat base is crumbly, place an individual serving plate on top of a ramekin when turning out the cheesecakes. Holding firmly, turn both over to invert. Carefully remove the ramekin and peel away the lining paper. Repeat for the remaining cheesecakes. Spoon the mango purée around each cheesecake and decorate the top of each with 3 raspberries, if using. Serve at once.

prepare in 15 mins

cooking time 5 mins + 3 hrs chilling

serves 4

ingredients

corn oil, for oiling

2 tbsp polyunsaturated spread

$^1/_2$ tsp ground ginger

$^5/_8$ cup rolled oats

1 large ripe mango, about
  1 lb 5 oz/600 g

$1^1/_8$ cups virtually fat-free
  Quark soft cheese

scant $^1/_2$ cup medium-fat
  soft cheese

12 raspberries, to decorate
  (optional)

Calories 287kcal	Fat 14.58g
Protein 12.9g	Saturates 5.79g
Carbohydrate 27.9g	Fiber 3.84g
Sugar 17.4g	Salt 0.33g

blueberry fools

prepare in 10 mins
cooking time 10 mins +
cooling
serves 4

ingredients

1 heaping tbsp custard powder

1¹/₄ cups skim or semiskim milk

2 tbsp superfine sugar

scant ³/₄ cup fresh or frozen
blueberries,
thawed if frozen

⁷/₈ cup lowfat mascarpone
cheese

1 Blend the custard powder with ¹/₄ cup of the milk in a heatproof bowl. Bring the remaining milk to a boil in a small pan and pour over the custard mixture, mixing well. Return the custard to the pan and return to a boil over medium–low heat, stirring constantly, until thickened. Pour the custard into the bowl and sprinkle the sugar over the top of the custard to prevent a skin forming. Cover and let cool completely.

2 Set aside 12 blueberries for decoration. Put the remaining blueberries and cold custard into a blender and process until smooth.

3 Spoon the mascarpone cheese and blueberry mixture in alternate layers into 4 tall glasses. Decorate with the reserved blueberries and serve at once.

Calories 136kcal	Fat 1.42g
Protein 6.8g	Saturates 0.86g
Carbohydrate 25.7g	Fiber 1.36g
Sugar 19.9g	Salt 0.18g

strawberry mousse

1 Drain the tofu and place in a food processor or blender.

2 Coarsely chop the strawberries and put in the food processor. Reserve some of the orange zest strips for decoration, and put the remaining zest in the food processor with the honey.

3 Process until smooth, then spoon into dessert dishes and chill in the refrigerator.

4 Decorate with the reserved orange zest.

prepare in 5 mins + chilling

cooking time 0 mins

serves 4

ingredients

8 oz/225 g silken tofu

1 lb/450 g ripe strawberries, hulled, washed, and dried

zest of 1 orange

1 tsp honey

Calories 77kcal	Fat 2.48g
Protein 5.5g	Saturates 0.28g
Carbohydrate 8.7g	Fiber 1.24g
Sugar 8.5g	Salt 0.02g

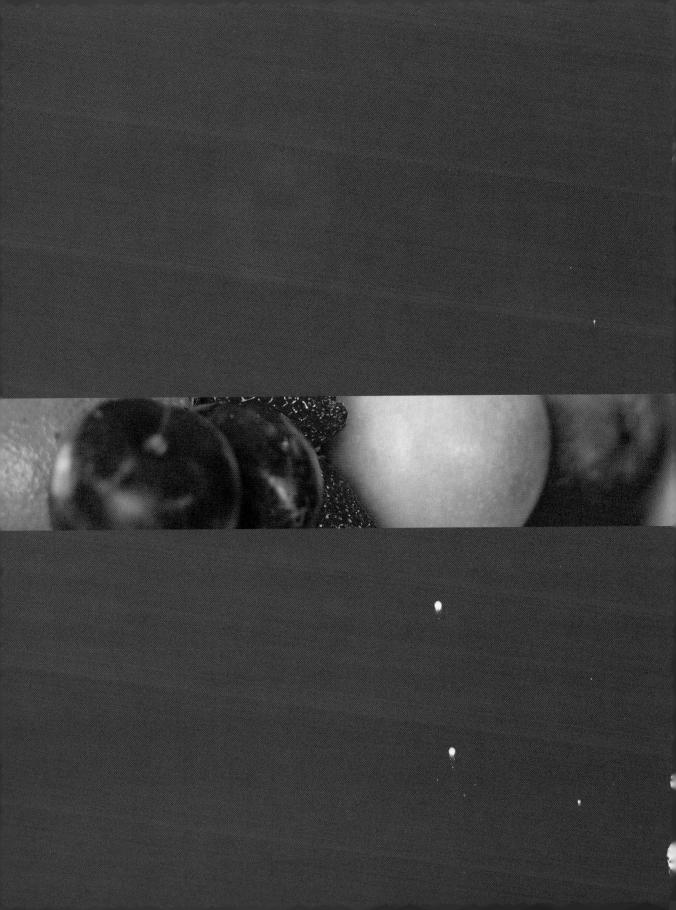

healthier treats

summer fruit slush

prepare in 5 mins
cooking time 0 mins
serves 2

ingredients

4 tbsp orange juice

1 tbsp lime juice

scant $^1/_2$ cup sparkling water

2$^1/_3$ cups frozen summer fruits
(such as blueberries,
raspberries, blackberries, and
strawberries)

4 ice cubes

DECORATION

fresh whole raspberries and
blackberries on a toothpick

1 Pour the orange juice,
lime juice, and sparkling
water into a food processor
and process gently until
combined.

2 Add the summer fruits
and ice cubes
and process until a slushy
consistency
has been reached.

3 Pour the mixture into
glasses, then decorate with whole raspberries and blackberries on
toothpicks and serve.

Calories 59kcal	Fat 0.21g
Protein 1.6g	Saturates 0.00g
Carbohydrate 13.3g	Fiber 1.96g
Sugar 13.3g	Salt 0.03g

banana & strawberry smoothie

1 Put the banana, strawberries, and yogurt into a blender and process for a few seconds until smooth.

2 Pour into a glass and serve at once.

prepare in 5 mins
cooking time 0 mins
serves 1

ingredients

1 banana, sliced

$^{1}/_{2}$ cup fresh strawberries, hulled

generous $^{2}/_{3}$ cup lowfat plain
  yogurt

Calories 202kcal	Fat 1.89g
Protein 9.1g	Saturates 1.09g
Carbohydrate 39.4g	Fiber 2.04g
Sugar 36.7g	Salt 0.26g

mixed vegetable bruschetta

prepare in 15 mins
cooking time 9 mins
serves 4

ingredients

olive oil, for brushing
and drizzling
1 red bell pepper, halved
and seeded
1 orange bell pepper, halved
and seeded
4 thick slices baguette
or ciabatta
1 red onion, sliced
1 fennel bulb, sliced
2 zucchini, sliced diagonally
2 garlic cloves, halved
1 tomato, halved
salt and pepper
fresh sage leaves,
to garnish

1 Brush the electric grill with oil and preheat. Cut each bell pepper half lengthwise into 4 strips. Toast the bread slices on both sides in a toaster or under a broiler.

2 When the grill is hot add the bell peppers and fennel and cook for 4 minutes, then add the onion and zucchini, and cook for 5 minutes more until all the vegetables are tender but still with a slight "bite." If necessary, cook the vegetables in 2 batches, as they should be placed on the grill in a single layer.

3 Meanwhile, rub the garlic halves over the toasts, then rub them with the tomato halves. Place on warm plates. Pile the grilled vegetables on top of the toasts, drizzle with olive oil, and season with salt and pepper. Garnish with sage leaves and serve warm.

Calories 242kcal	Fat 10.54g
Protein 7.3g	Saturates 1.52g
Carbohydrate 31.6g	Fiber 5.29g
Sugar 10.6g	Salt 0.58g

mixed sushi rolls

1 Put the rice into a pan and cover with cold water. Bring to a boil, then reduce the heat, cover, and let simmer for 15–20 minutes, or until the rice is tender and the water has been absorbed. Drain if necessary and transfer to a bowl. Mix the vinegar, sugar and salt together, then, using a spatula, stir well into the rice. Cover with a damp cloth and let cool.

2 To make the rolls, lay a clean bamboo mat over a cutting board. Lay a sheet of nori, shiny side-down, on the mat. Spread a quarter of the rice mixture over the nori, using wet fingers to press it down evenly, leaving a 1/2-inch/1-cm margin at the top and bottom.

3 For smoked salmon and cucumber rolls, lay the salmon over the rice and arrange the cucumber in a line across the center. For the shrimp rolls, lay the shrimp and avocado in a line across the center.

4 Carefully hold the nearest edge of the mat, then, using the mat as a guide, roll up the nori tightly to make a neat tube of rice enclosing the filling. Seal the uncovered edge with a little water, then roll the sushi off the mat. Repeat to make 3 more rolls—you need 2 salmon and cucumber and 2 shrimp and avocado in total.

5 Using a wet knife, cut each roll into 8 pieces and stand upright on a platter. Wipe and rinse the knife between cuts to prevent the rice sticking. Serve the rolls with wasabi, tamari, and pickled ginger.

prepare in 20 mins

cooking time 25 mins + cooling

serves 4 as a snack

ingredients

4 sheets nori (seaweed) for rolling

RICE

scant 1 1/4 cups sushi rice

2 tbsp rice vinegar

1 tsp superfine sugar

1/2 tsp salt

FILLINGS

1 3/4 oz/50 g smoked salmon

1 1/2-inch/4-cm piece cucumber, peeled, seeded, and cut into short thin sticks

1 1/2 oz/40 g cooked shelled shrimp

1 small avocado, pitted, peeled, thinly sliced, and tossed in lemon juice

TO SERVE

wasabi (Japanese horseradish sauce)

tamari (wheat-free soy sauce)

pink pickled ginger

Calories 326kcal	Fat 7.52g
Protein 13.8g	Saturates 1.32g
Carbohydrate 48.8g	Fiber 5.44g
Sugar 1.6g	Salt 0.63g

quick mackerel pâté

prepare in 10 mins +
chilling
cooking time 0 mins
serves 4

ingredients

9 oz/250 g skinless smoked
mackerel fillets
generous 2/3 cup lowfat plain
yogurt
1 tbsp chopped fresh parsley
1 tbsp lemon juice
finely grated rind of 1/2 lemon
freshly ground black pepper
TO GARNISH
4 lemon wedges
few sprigs of fresh parsley
1 red bell pepper, seeded and cut
into chunky strips
TO SERVE
1 yellow bell pepper, seeded and
cut into chunky strips
2 carrots, cut into strips
2 celery stalks, cut into strips
slices whole-wheat or white
bread, toasted and
cut into triangles

1 Remove and discard any remaining bones from the mackerel fillets and put the fish into a small bowl. Mash the fish with a fork and combine with the yogurt, parsley, and lemon juice and rind. Season to taste with pepper.

2 Divide the pâté between 4 ramekins. Cover and let chill until required or serve at once.

3 To serve, garnish the pâté with lemon wedges and parsley sprigs and serve with the prepared vegetables and toasted bread.

Calories 281kcal	Fat 20.09g
Protein 14.8g	Saturates 4.27g
Carbohydrate 10.8g	Fiber 2.49g
Sugar 10.3g	Salt 1.31g

Yogurt & Cucumber Dip

1 Peel then coarsely grate the cucumber. Put in a sieve and squeeze out as much of the water as possible. Put the cucumber into a bowl.

2 Add the yogurt, garlic, and chopped mint (reserve a little as a garnish, if desired) to the cucumber and season with pepper. Mix well together and chill in the refrigerator for about 2 hours before serving.

3 To serve, stir the cucumber and yogurt dip and transfer to a serving bowl. Sprinkle with salt and accompany with warmed pita bread if using.

prepare in 10 mins + chilling

cooking time 0 mins

serves 4

ingredients

1 small cucumber

1¼ cups authentic Greek Yogurt

1 large garlic clove, crushed

1 tbsp chopped fresh mint or dill

salt and pepper

warm pita bread, to serve
  (optional)

Calories 45kcal	Fat 0.78g
Protein 3.8g	Saturates 0.5g
Carbohydrate 6.1g	Fiber 0.2g
Sugar 5.7g	Salt 0.12g

Golden Raisin Tealoaf

prepare in 5 mins +
1 - 8 hrs chilling

cooking time
40 - 45 mins

makes one 1 lb/450 g
loaf—10 – 12 slices

ingredients

corn oil, for oiling

scant ¹/₂ cup bran flakes

²/₃ cup golden raisins

scant ¹/₂ cup firmly packed raw
brown sugar

1¹/₄ cups skim or semiskim milk

scant 1¹/₂ cups self-rising flour

tea or freshly squeezed
fruit juice,
to serve

1 Very lightly oil a 1-lb/450-g loaf pan and line the bottom with waxed paper.

2 Put the bran flakes, golden raisins, sugar, and milk into a mixing bowl, cover, and let soak for at least 1 hour in the refrigerator, or until the bran flakes have softened and the fruit has plumped up after absorbing some of the milk—the mixture can be left overnight in the refrigerator.

3 Preheat the oven to 375°F/190°C. Stir the flour into the soaked ingredients, mix well, and spoon into the loaf pan. Bake in the preheated oven for 40–45 minutes, or until the point of a sharp knife inserted into the center of the loaf comes out clean. Let cool in the pan on a wire rack.

4 When cold, turn the loaf out, and discard the lining paper. Serve in slices with cups of tea or glasses of freshly squeezed fruit juice. Store any leftover loaf in an airtight container and consume within 2–3 days.

Calories 161kcal	Fat 1.2g
Protein 3.6g	Saturates 0.41g
Carbohydrate 36.3g	Fiber 1.37g
Sugar 19.5g	Salt 0.3g

fruit & nut squares

1 Preheat the oven to 350°F/180°C. Lightly grease a 7-inch/18-cm shallow, square baking pan with butter. Beat the remaining butter with the honey in a bowl until creamy, then beat in the egg with the almonds.

2 Add the remaining ingredients and mix together. Press into the prepared pan, ensuring that the mixture is firmly packed. Smooth the top.

3 Bake in the preheated oven for 20–25 minutes, or until firm to the touch and golden brown.

4 Remove from the oven and let stand for 10 minutes before marking into squares. Let stand until cold before removing from the pan. Store in an airtight container.

prepare in 10 mins
cooking time 20 - 25 mins
+ 10 mins chilling
makes 9 squares

ingredients

4 oz/115 g unsalted butter,
   plus extra for greasing
2 tbsp honey
1 egg, beaten
scant $7/8$ cup ground almonds
$7/8$ cup no-soak dried apricots,
   finely chopped
$1/3$ cup dried cherries
scant $3/8$ cup toasted chopped
   hazelnuts
$1/8$ cup sesame seeds
scant 1 cup rolled oats

Calories 310kcal	Fat 23.41g
Protein 6.0g	Saturates 8.35g
Carbohydrate 20.0g	Fiber 2.82g
Sugar 12.8g	Salt 0.05g

carrot bars

prepare in 10 mins
cooking time 35 - 45 mins
+ cooling
makes 14 – 16 bars

ingredients

corn oil, for oiling

6 oz/175 g unsalted butter

generous 3/8 cup (packed) brown sugar

2 eggs, beaten

scant 1/2 cup self-rising whole-wheat flour, sifted

1 tsp baking powder, sifted

1 tsp ground cinnamon, sifted

generous 11/8 cups ground almonds

4 oz/115 g carrot, coarsely grated

1/2 cup golden raisins

1/2 cup no-soak dried apricots, finely chopped

scant 3/8 cup toasted chopped hazelnuts

1 tbsp slivered almonds

1 Preheat the oven to 350°F/180°C. Lightly oil and line a 10- x 8-inch/25- x 20-cm shallow, rectangular baking pan with nonstick parchment paper.

2 Cream the butter and sugar together in a bowl until light and fluffy, then gradually beat in the eggs, adding a little flour after each addition.

3 Add all the remaining ingredients, except the slivered almonds. Spoon the mixture into the prepared pan and smooth the top. Sprinkle with the slivered almonds.

4 Bake in the preheated oven for 35–45 minutes, or until the mixture is cooked and a skewer inserted into the center comes out clean.

5 Remove from the oven and let cool in the pan. Remove from the pan, discard the lining paper, and cut into bars.

Calories 221kcal	Fat 16.75g
Protein 4.0g	Saturates 6.69g
Carbohydrate 14.6g	Fiber 1.72g
Sugar 12.1g	Salt 0.14g

index